Longman Resources for Writers

A Guide for Peer Response
Second Edition

by
Tori Haring-Smith

Revised and Expanded by Helon H. Raines
Armstrong Atlantic State University

 **LONGMAN**

An imprint of Addison Wesley Longman, Inc.

New York • Reading, Massachusetts • Menlo Park, California • Harlow, England
Don Mills, Ontario • Sydney • Mexico City • Madrid • Amsterdam

Editor-in-Chief: Patricia Rossi
Supplements Editor: Donna Campion

ISBN 0-321-01948-2

345678910—CB—00

TABLE OF CONTENTS

Section I

Introductory Materials

INTRODUCTION

As an early beneficiary of Tori Haring-Smith's *Student Manual for Peer Evaluation,* I welcome the opportunity to contribute to an expanded guide for developing writing/learning communities in introductory composition courses. Retaining Haring-Smith's original forms for peer evaluation and adding commentary and supplemental response sheets, the new edition reflects current, and common, practices among experienced composition instructors who employ a workshop approach to improve student reading, writing, speaking, listening and critical thinking skills. Based on the premise that developing effective writing groups in the composition class means teaching basic strategies for effective response, the resource includes the following new items:

- comments to instructors
- comments to students
- response forms, new to this edition, addressed to specific contexts
- evaluation forms to monitor individual and group response processes
- additional materials about writing groups

The **comments to instructors (I. B.)** are addressed primarily to teachers with limited experience in designing student-centered composition courses. These notes are an introduction to peer response as a key element in writing processes and a central aspect of the writing workshop, itself a basic structure in collaborative learning in composition courses. Like writing, critiquing texts consists of multiple processes that evolve and change according to context. Thus, effective response results when basic assumptions about reading, writing, speaking, listening, and thinking undergird classroom activities. The purpose of the notes to instructors then is to comment on common issues and principles in designing and developing response groups.

The **purpose of the notes to students (I.C.)** is to assist novice peer respondents in understanding the purposes and procedures so that they use the materials in Section III not as ends in themselves but as ways to create constructive and diplomatic dialogue.

If used in conjunction with Chapters Two and Three of Haring-Smith's *Learning Together: An Introduction to Collaborative Learning* and with Section 2-e of *The Little, Brown Handbook,* the response materials (III.) of *Resources* provide directions and activities to alter the dynamics of the writing class. Haring-Smith's original evaluation forms and the new note sheets and response forms offer ways to engage students in conversations that focus on creating texts to achieve specific purposes for audiences beyond the teacher and the group. These forms also may assist instructors in fulfilling our roles as experienced readers acting first as coaches and ultimately as evaluators of numerous pages of texts generated in composition classes.

Reflective practice and accountability enhance collaborative endeavors. Therefore, *Resources* also

→

provides sample forms for students to evaluate both individual and group responses and processes (III.C.). Finally, a list of **additional materials useful to instructors (IV)** completes the resource manual.

Peer response can be an effective tool for improving student writing and also can assist instructors in providing useful commentary on those processes and products. The materials included here have been created, tested, and revised by composition teachers and students over a period of ten years. However, modifications to better meet the purposes of specific reading and writing situations are appropriate, even essential, to achieve the goals of any writing/learning community.

Helon Raines
Associate Professor, Department of English
Armstrong Atlantic State University
Savannah, Georgia
July, 1997

NOTES TO INSTRUCTORS

- **The Situation:** You've heard about it; you've seen it; maybe you've used peer response in your classes. Most likely, if you were a graduate assistant in the last fifteen years, you've been instructed in the method and either are an advocate or a limited user. Peer response has been a popular topic at conferences, in professional development workshops, and in composition journals. Beginning teachers, therefore, could assume that in a "post-process" period college students already have learned how to dialogue with peer readers as one aspect of developing a text. So what do instructors need to know about peer response to teach college English courses today?

- **The Experience:** Perhaps not too much, although my experience suggests otherwise. From 1976 until 1994, teaching full time in a two-year college, I also offered upper-level courses in a university extension program. Since 1994, I have taught in a four-year state college/university in a different region of the country. Beginning around 1986, I started to question students about their experiences with collaborative methodology, in general, process writing, and peer response, or group work, in particular. In a typical first-term class of 25 people, I may find two or three who have participated in writing groups, and, in a second-term course, five or six. Of those who profess a conscious recognition of some aspects of their writing processes, almost none understands a concept of audience and purpose besides those of the teacher who will assign a grade. Such an unscientific assessment of how thoroughly or how frequently writing is taught as a set of various processes obviously does not offer reliable or conclusive evidence. Nonetheless, these informal surveys of students, as well as conversations with colleagues around the country, constitute the basis for my contention that, while much has been said about teaching processes and about having multiple audiences respond before student texts go to intended readers, actual classroom practice is far more limited.

- **The Problem:** Therefore, references to "post-process" make me feel as if I am looking into a funhouse mirror. In the years I've taught writing, of course, this is not the first time I've realized that another decade or so must past before thinking among leading compositionists will be reflected in the institutions where I teach. However, the idea that the paradigm of process writing has reached universal acceptance seems particularly problematic because for some it could imply that we no longer need to teach college students methods for creating reader-based prose. Yet, that view would be a serious distortion of reality in many two-year and smaller four-year colleges and universities located between the coasts of California and the academic centers of the Northeast, those less progressive institutions where the majority of students take composition. In fact, to assume most college students are well versed in invention strategies, discovery writing, dialogue as dialectic, conversation as critique, and audience response as critical to the construction of text, from initial thoughts to edited product, is illusion of the highest order. From that perspective, we might concede that our colleagues who refused to teach generation strategies, invite

→

multiple drafts, or require revisions were the ones with the greatest clarity of vision. Did they foresee that soon students entering college would be experienced, if not accomplished, in all aspects of composing written discourse, just as they were in decades past? And have we now reached that time? Obviously, I think not. I stress this point because those who have taught primarily in research universities may find that the assumptions made there aren't valid in colleges where most English faculty positions are available. Furthermore, the amount of untutored writing that instructors read makes the use of peer response groups more important for a process pedagogy and also makes teaching students how to respond assume greater significance.

- **The Audience for these Notes:** These notes then are addressed to instructors in colleges and universities heavily populated by re-entry students. In these places, "traditional," students quite often attended high schools where the cutting edge rarely made a mark in the product approach and/or where even those teachers enlightened by regional writing projects or recertification courses either burned out or were burned up as the unwanted messengers of tidings from a world too far from local reality. These notes also are addressed to those who want to know more but have limited time to investigate the extensive literature (a list of additional resources appears in Section IV), as well as to those who tried response groups years ago and either abandoned them or employ them in limited ways but want to revisit the practice.

- **The Purpose of the Notes:** I offer these notes as the compilation of my personal reading, experimentation, trial and error, theft, and vandalization—one practitioner's strategies that often have made my classes more effective. These "tips" also are offered with the usual caveat that nothing here is guaranteed to work. As is true of most writing teachers, I have not taught a class in which the methods were completely successful with every student. However, at least to my knowledge, no method promises 100% effectiveness, and peer response as part of a workshop class has improved student writing enough in my classes that I remain committed to the practice.

→

PREMISES

Peer response

- is a basic method of the collaborative class and the writing workshop and is integral to a process theory of writing,
- works best when integrated with other practices that enhance creation of a writing/learning community,
- is itself a set of processes that must be learned,
- is particularly appropriate in writing classes that emphasize audience awareness and analysis,
- is structured, although experienced groups may determine their own structures,
- helps writers create reader-based prose when used during as many stages of the writing process as logistically possible,
- is not the only response an assignment receives (although in some phases of the process it may be the primary and most thorough response),
- is an activity to teach students not just about writing but also about reading, listening, taking notes, writing summaries, and dialoguing, developing verbal abilities in general and an ability to talk about writing specifically,
- takes some amount of classroom time to teach, to implement, and to assess.

ADVANTAGES FOR STUDENTS

Peer response

- helps students develop a sense of audience,
- teaches the value of multiple audiences,
- aids in building the writing/learning community,
- creates a more student-centered class,
- makes students more responsible for their learning,
- creates groups that continue to meet outside of class,
- teaches that effective communication is a reward in itself,
- comes naturally to many students,
- is an activity most students enjoy,
- provides every student the opportunity to think and to talk about writing,
- helps students internalize effective strategies of writing,
- teaches students how to participate in negotiations that enhance team performance,
- helps students better understand assignments, instructions,
- improves listening and note-taking skills,
- allows writers to gain distance on their own texts,
- provides experiences that demonstrate how a reader participates in creating meaning in any text and also how knowledge is socially constructed.

→

ADVANTAGES TO THE TEACHER

Peer Response
- may reduce the amount the teacher needs to comment (It is especially rewarding when the teacher can say simply, "I agree with your readers."),
- helps the teacher assume the role of coach rather than be assigned the role of enemy,
- improves the quality of writing, as well as other skills, and makes the latter segment of the course more enjoyable,
- may be evaluated by the level of independence groups achieve (While it is not the goal, a measure of success is when groups need little, if any, supervision, for instance, when I can attend a conference without getting a substitute. On the other hand, I do have classes that never get to the point I'd leave them alone. Furthermore, I do encourage instructors to be active in overseeing group work until groups have proven themselves to do better when left alone.).

COMMON STRUCTURES

The Groups
- usually are made up of three or five students (five is considered ideal but must be varied depending on the amount of time the group has for response),
- may be organized through various methods: random selection (numbering off, seating proximity, arrival time); teacher assignment (based on similarities and/or differences in personalities, levels of performance, interests, majors, topics, ages, genders, ethnicity); self-selection,
- change during the term, particularly in the first composition course; this has significant advantages among inexperienced peer respondents, but assigning groups for the term can work in some classes,
- work better with assigned roles, which rotate; common ones are coordinator (time-keeper, facilitator); note-keeper; observer (of response processes); presenter (to report on group activities and processes),
- are evaluated by the teacher in some defined ways (review of notes, respondent forms, oral presentations, observation).

COMMON PROCEDURES INCLUDE THE FOLLOWING:
- One student reads her or his paper aloud to the group at least once (teaches students listening and note-taking skills; most important, authors experience the value of the technique for revising and editing).
- Papers are read twice (some readings may be outside of class and by a respondent one time)
- each respondent comments orally.
- Beginning respondents write-either on the response forms and/or on respondents' note sheets (samples included in Sections II and III.)
- One respondent summarizes the group's collective comments for the author (and for the teacher to review).

→

- Or respondents give their notes and summary sentences to the author.
- Students provide hard-copy for readers at editing stages; for the second reading of any draft; or in classes where papers are read outside of class or via E-mail allows author to reread commentary later and gives respondents practice in reading even though it does not give practice in listening and in speaking.
- Authors comment only at specific points in the process, usually at the end to ask or answer questions or at the beginning to describe audience, purpose, revisions.

STRATEGIES FOR TEACHING PEER RESPONSE
The teacher
- has an experienced group "model" the practice (some writing centers provide this service),
- shows videos that demonstrate processes (see reference list, Section IV, for suggestions),
- models or discusses the "ideal" peer respondent after reviewing the "types" (see "Notes to Students," I. C.),
- discusses criteria for effective response and good processes,
- assigns a "practice" session with all groups reading and responding to the same paper (one provided by the instructor or one in *The Little, Brown Handbook*),
- participates as a respondent in one group to model for the whole class, or sits in each group occasionally to model, to comment on other responses and/or to adjust group composition,
- uses groups' written critiques and/or oral reports as a basis for discussing purposes, problems, solutions,
- encourages students to use the writing center and to note how tutors question and comment (also stresses the value of multiple audiences),
- stresses the importance of taking notes and of completing peer response forms, especially until respondents become experienced,
- shows students ways to balance time so that conversation always is the priority; as groups advance, eliminates required paper work to stress that the forms are means to an end,
- provides forms that contain fewer questions as groups converse more freely.

COMMON PROBLEMS
Students
- have done "group work" and think they know what to do,
- think peer response is "busy work," a time for teachers to take a break and for students to take it easy,
- assume inappropriate roles: are blunt, negative, controlling, or, more frequently, fear being critical because they don't want to hurt feelings and/or want to protect their own writing from criticism, or apologize, self-criticize, socialize, in general get "off topic" and produce little substantive commentary,
- race through reading, writing, critiquing to "get it done" (often hoping as soon as they "finish"

→

they can leave class or at least sit back and shoot the breeze),
- spend all the time filling out the forms; no conversation ensues (for first sessions this may be necessary and in some cases may be all the instructor wants),
- are absent on workshop days (fearing to expose their writing or thinking only the teacher's comments matter),
- show up without a draft or come late (with heart-wrenching stories of computer breakdowns and missing disks),
- are too shy to speak (as respondent or as author); are too hostile to hear their readers' comments; don't listen well; don't learn enough about good writing to comment appropriately,
- are concerned about mechanics when major construction problems should be the priority,
- allow one person to dominate or one to do most of the work, or, the opposite, allow some to do little or nothing,
- group themselves according to ability and resist changing groups; thus good students are with good students leaving weaker students together (sometimes this may be the best arrangement, particularly if the teacher works closely with the latter).

SOME SOLUTIONS
Response often improves if the teacher
- considers the writing/learning community as a total concept; each aspect of the method must be carefully organized, introduced, and sequenced,
- begins instruction in the concept and the methodology the first day, at least the first week; emphasizes the significance in the syllabus through statements of purposes, methods, and assignment schedules that indicate group work dates and activities,
- has an attendance policy or, better, gets the class, or each group, to set its own rules about attendance, notification of absence, tardiness, late work,
- lets students know very clearly, very early that beginning peer response groups do not evaluate the writing assignments for grades *or*
- lets them know when and how peer response and self-evaluation will count on the grade
- provides information about available computer technology,
- begins class activities with a group project, such as introducing another student,
- provides a class directory of phone numbers (with students' permission, of course),
- makes an early assignment in a professional text that guides students through small group discussion about that writing before they start working with one another's texts,
- keeps members of the initial groups together for one professional text discussion and for at least two drafts of the first writing assignment so a group rapport develops and so respondents comment on initial drafts and revisions,
- is open to students' problems and allows respondents to modify the process,
- violates any of these principles rather than do anything that gets in the way of the ultimate goal— students talking productively about their own writing by first learning to talk critically about the writing of their peers, as well as about writing in professional texts,

→

OTHER SUGGESTIONS

Productivity and participation improve through accountability because

- respondents use individual respondent evaluation forms,
- teacher recognizes particularly effective response groups and/or students identified as strong respondents. (To find out who these students are, ask, "If you could choose only one person to work with again, who would that be and why?"),
- teacher provides feedback from authors to individuals at mid-term; provides instructor evaluation of each group and of individual members' strengths and weaknesses.

MISCELLANY

AN EARLY ASSIGNMENT:

A good opening assignment is for students to interview each other and introduce their partner to the class. (We sit in a circle and repeat names and identifying characteristics until someone can name everyone and all of us have said everyone's name several times.) The interview notes become the basis for the first out-of-class writing assignment, which is a feature article published in a *Student Interviews* booklet. This assignment works well to teach skills needed to accomplish many of the goals of collaborative learning and shows students generation strategies and revision. One of the goals is to build trust among the students, to establish early that the group approach is for support, to help each other learn and improve. It also quickly demonstrates the problems when students don't attend class regularly and don't do their assignments on schedule. This publication doesn't appear until products are relatively error-free (which emphasizes the "product" standard for the course). Therefore, the book often is published late in the course; however, at that point, it documents the community the class has become. In addition, it gives most students a sense of what it means to create a public writing; it immediately provides experience in writing for an audience besides the teacher; it reminds them of who they were and how they wrote at the beginning of the class; it heightens their awareness of writing and learning as an ongoing and social process.

ON AN EARLY ASSIGNMENT IN THE PROFESSIONAL TEXT:

Another practice that contributes to building the writing/learning community is for students to collaborate in studying the professional texts, whether stories, essays, or the handbook. That group activity, before any peer response on students' writings, establishes the importance of team efforts. A write-to-learn exercise, such as journals or quick in-class responses, give practice in reading informal writings aloud. If students remain in the same group for the first out-of-class essay, the members usually are moderately comfortable with one another and with sharing their thoughts and their writings.

WHEN TO PRESENT MODELS OF EFFECTIVE RESPONSE GROUPS:

Sometimes the first peer response session is before students see demonstrations of model groups.

→

After struggling through a session, respondents may be more willing to learn from the models. A writing exercise that asks for ways to improve their group work is the basis for class discussion about the concept and the practice (sample "meditation" on the following page). The class may develop a picture of the "ideal" respondent" and the "receptive author" (see exercises in I.C. "Notes to Students"). The teacher allows time at the end of the first couple of response sessions for each group to report on its process and progress, what the group did better, what still needs work. This always results in improvement in the next sessions.

Explicit instructions in "what to do," either for a response session before the demonstrations or for the first session following, allow students to review the pointers and variations on the processes and thus serve as a supplemental text on peer response (sample instruction sheets provided in Section II).

ADDITIONAL USEFUL MATERIALS AVAILABLE WITH THE HANDBOOK

Having students read the handbook about response is a good preliminary assignment to early sessions. Particularly helpful in *The Little, Brown Handbook* is Section 1c on "Audience," pages 30–35; section 2e, pages 80–84; as well as the Introduction, "Critical Thinking, Reading, and Writing," pages 1–21. Having students respond to the sample student paper and compare those to the model in the text provides a good practice session.

Materials in Chapter Two of *Learning Together* also help students understand the process, the roles, the negotiations, the potential conflicts and resolutions. Materials in Chapter Three of *Learning Together* help students improve their dialogue and their written comments.

SAMPLE QUIZ FOLLOWING DEMONSTRATION OF A MODEL GROUP

Meditation—Respond to the following on your own paper.

1. What was the topic of the paper in the demonstration?

2. What is the one comment you agreed with about the paper?

3. One with which you disagreed?

4. What is one thing your group does that is the same as the more experienced group?

5. What is one thing they did that your group doesn't?

6. What is one thing you saw in the demonstration you will try?

7. How were these respondents able to say so much?

8. What did the writer do while the respondents talked?

☜

NOTES TO STUDENTS

ARE YOU A PDSA (PERFECT DRAFT STRATEGY ADDICT)?
DON'T KNOW? TAKE THIS QUIZ TO FIND OUT.

YES   NO

1. Do you put off starting to write an assignment until the night before it is due, or, at the most, a few days before?
2. Do you avoid reading the assignment sheet carefully (or at all) until you sit down to write the first (and possibly only) draft?
3. Do you frequently stay up all night to finish a writing assignment?
4. Do you anguish over every word before you put it down?
5. Do you worry about each mark of punctuation and every spelling at the same time you are composing the whole text?
6. Is it usually too late for anyone to read your paper before you turn it in?
7. Do you seldom have time to reread the paper, even for minor editing?
8. Do you make excuses to yourself or others about your essay, such as not liking the topic, hating to write essays, being bored with the class, disliking the teacher, or the teacher disliking you?
9. Do you pretend, to yourself or others, that you are indifferent to the consequences ("Oh, I just dashed this off right before class.")?
10. Then do you cry, scream, curse, or otherwise "act out," in your mind or in reality, when the paper comes back with a disappointing evaluation?
11. Do you promise whenever any of the above happens you'll start earlier next time?

TOTAL

Self Diagnosis: Count the "yes" responses. If the total is:

1–3—you know what to do, although you may not always do it;

4–8—you need help;

9+—rush to the nearest control center for PDS addiction.

   (And there *is* help nearby.)

→

- **The Problem with Perfect Draft Addiction:** Some of you probably have done well on past writing assignments using the perfect draft strategy. This may occur when documents are short enough, if you know enough about the topics, if the assignment has one or two purposes to accomplish to get a high evaluation, if the teacher isn't concerned with how you write, so long as you do the assignment, and/or if you have spent your writing life practicing PDS. In fact, some writing situations do call for a "final" reader-based draft in a short period of time, things such as entry and exit writing assessments, some diagnostic essays, short memos, quick notes and letters, and journalistic news reports. In any of these cases, however, writers who have learned several invention, organizing, drafting, revising, and editing processes, can apply those to produce polished texts that communicate more effectively to the reader. These writers use a revision process in whatever time is available. However, the above situations are not the only ones, or even the most common ones, in college classes or in your future employment. Therefore, students find it advantageous to develop approaches besides PDS to solve writing problems, no matter who the audience is or what the task entails.

  In the future, you will write for various audiences and purposes and in different forms. One or two writing classes cannot teach you all of those. Upper-level classes in your major may expose you to specific conventions of the discipline, and on-the-job experience will provide immediate training. Therefore, many college composition courses focus on developing various writing processes so you have multiple strategies to draw on when you must write in situations with which you have little past experience.

- **The Effect of Peer Response on Writing Processes:** One advantage of peer response in composition is to provide writers insight into how a communication affects readers. Another outcome may be to get you in the habit of starting sooner. If the teacher allows, or requires, several drafts of the same essay, then you must begin working on the assignment a week or so before the final due date. Even though you still may procrastinate until the last minute for the early drafts, ideally it won't be long before you start sooner simply because you don't want to subject your peers to hearing you stumble through materials to which you've obviously given little time or thought. As a respondent, you quickly learn how difficult it is to work with a text that has been thrown together just so the author has a draft. (This is also why it's probably best not to tell respondents that you wrote this right before class, something that usually is apparent, but which also says to the group, "I'm not concerned about how difficult I've made it for you to help me with this draft.")

  Of course, even when you have given time to a first draft, often it still is fairly rough. At least when that occurs, you have the opportunity to talk with your preliminary readers about the assignment, to go over what you were trying to do that isn't working. What seems salvageable to them and to you? What is interesting or contains elements worth pursuing? What can your readers suggest to help you get closer to the assignment requirements or to your intended goals? You let them know that the poverty of the text isn't due to lack of respect for them, and you also can then practice one of the best generation strategies around.

→

- **Dialogue as Generation:** Dialogue is an excellent form of getting ideas for topics, for getting started, and certainly for revising. If you have been a member of a serious study group, you already know the value of several brains working together. While you don't want someone to tell you what to think on your paper topic, hearing what others think about the subject can give you ideas, refine your own thoughts, and also allows you to experience various responses and interpretations you might get from a "real" audience. Then you can make adjustments accordingly. Things we never think about come out when we listen to the questions of someone who has listened carefully to our text. Just reading our text aloud allows us to hear problems we don't see when we read silently. Furthermore, most of us do hear ourselves talk in our heads (which is not the same thing as hearing "voices," although neither talking to ourselves silently or aloud or hearing voices necessarily indicates a mental disturbance unless all good writers are mentally disturbed, a point more appropriately debated elsewhere). But hearing ourselves say things aloud to others frequently has the happy effect of clarifying our thinking. This may be the reason the famous saying, "How do I know what I think until I see what I've said," could be expanded to "*and* hear what I've said I think."

- **Peer Process for Early Drafts:** So early drafts are to discover how your text affects one audience, a few of your peers, as well as how your thinking affects you when you hear it read from your own lips to other people. Then your teacher also may comment and thus you have lots of ideas for revising. Or, if your teacher doesn't read early drafts, then you have the opportunity to make changes before the paper is graded. One thing to remember about response on early drafts, however, is that this is not a time to comment on, or ask for advise about, refinements in syntax or diction and certainly not on spelling and punctuation except as those might affect the revision (as in consistently misspelling one of the common words of the topic or an awkward phrasing that will be used several times). The awkward sentences, including their misleading directions to readers because of faulty punctuation, may not even be in the next draft. The purpose of the early draft response is to look at overall ideas, organization, development for coherence, sufficiency, validity. Because initially group members may think that revising is editing and as respondents can find errors in spelling and punctuation where they may not know how to talk about substantive composing issues, groups often take valuable time to edit materials that will be cut in revision. Save editing and stylistic revisions for the next draft (unless, of course, the writer has already taken the paper through multiple drafts). Some teachers will devote one peer response session to editing only.

- **Some common issues:** Students sometimes have had negative experiences with small groups. Indeed, some groups do not function well and end up being a waste of time for everyone. However, you can prevent this from being the case with peer response in this class. First, your teacher will provide materials to help you give and receive effective comments. One of these may be a demonstration of a peer response group after which you discuss some of your specific questions. One common question is what's in this for me? Some of the advantages of peer response are listed in the "Notes to the Instructor" on page 5 of this manual.

→

EXERCISE ONE

One way to identify potential problems and to iron out any misconceptions is to make a list of questions about group work to share with two or three members of the class. Comparing questions, you can compile a list of five or six of the common ones, or the most sensible ones, and then come up with some tentative answers or possible solutions. Then each group may read their solution to the rest of the class.

EXERCISE TWO

Another way to think about solving problems in small groups is to create some case studies. Your group then gives your case to the next group for them to solve, and you get some other group's case study. Compare cases and responses. Just remember these should be fictional case studies to protect the guilty.

THE PROBLEM

SAMPLE CASE STUDY:
One of the members of our group, Sue, someone we all like, is frequently absent on workshop days. If she does come to class, she often is late and we never know whether she will have a draft or not. Waiting to see whether or not she will show up makes us late getting started, so, if she does have a paper, we don't get to it until last when we are already short on time. Yet, if we start without her, then she doesn't hear the first reading of someone's paper. Any suggestions?

THE SOLUTION

How about some ground rules before the group starts to work?
Your Turn:

→

EXERCISE THREE

EXERCISE TO CONSTRUCT MODELS FOR PEER RESPONSE GROUP

I. To think about what a good peer respondent is:
1. Make a list of five reasons you don't want to do peer response.
2. Next make a list of five characteristics of someone you would trust to read and comment on your text.
3. List five things you hope no respondent would ever do or say in relation to your paper.
4. Construct a description of a model peer respondent.
5. Compare these lists with other people's in your class or group.

Now all of you look carefully at the models you've constructed. If the respondent behaves as you ask, how much help will you get in revising the text so it will be more effective for your final reader(s) or to improve the grade you will get on the final essay? With your group, you may now want to modify the example.

II. To think about the "Model" Author Listening to Peer Response:
1. Make a list of three things it would be most productive to do as the writer listening to members of your group respond to your paper.
2. Make a second list of at least three things that you might do that would be counter-productive.
3. Construct a profile, with members of your group, of the writer who will get the most out of comments from respondents.

III. Avoiding problems in peer groups.

If you've worked in groups before you may have encountered some of the problems when members of the group have not learned behaviors conducive to effective group interaction. List as many as you can of the "types" of students you have encountered or can imagine you might encounter. Describe the "type" respondent you have been or think you might be. (ie. "the little teacher" is a person who tells the writer what is wrong with the paper, often what is wrong with the mechanics and grammar, and what to do to "correct" the paper.) (If you can't think of any "types," look at the list at the bottom of page 21 and then describe what those people must do in groups that probably will hinder the progress of the team.)

Guidelines for Response

General Guidelines for Peer Respondents

Author's Name:_____

Respondents' Names:_____

Respondents may respond to the following questions as well as commenting directly on a copy of the paper. Each respondent may answer the questions or one reader may record the collective responses, noting by initials of the respondents where opinions differ. These forms may be completed outside of class; in-class; for E-mail response or in classes with networked computers. Your instructor will advise you of the process.

Carefully read, or listen to the paper being read, before making any comments. If the writer has a self-evaluation, read it *after* answering question 1.

1. Consider the thesis, purpose and audience for the paper. Are they indicated clearly? Are they consistent? If not, ask the writer questions to help clarify these essential elements of writing.

2. Skim the paper to see how it is organized. Are there any breaks in the organization? If so, try to explain why you feel that a gap exists. Whenever possible, phrase your comments as questions, not as judgments. If you think that the organization needs to be revised significantly, skip to question 7 after answering this question.

3. Now go back and look at each paragraph. Is it unified, coherent, and developed? If not, ask the writer a question to help focus or complete the paragraph.

4. Are the paragraphs connected to one another smoothly and logically? If there are only logical gaps between the paragraphs, ask the writer how one paragraph is linked to the next. If you think that most of the paragraphs need to be revised significantly, skip to question 7 after answering this question.

→

5. Now look at sentences. Do any sentences confuse you? If so, try to describe your confusion or ask the reader a question about the sentence.

6. Are there any mechanical or grammatical problems in the paper? If so point them out to the writer, but do not correct them.

7. Decide what the paper's two most important strengths are: Point these out to the writer.

8. Write a summary comment that begins by telling the writer what you think the thesis, purpose, and audience for the paper are. Then explain what you liked best about the paper. Finally, describe the two features of the paper that most need improvement. If you can, describe a strategy for overcoming these problems; do so briefly.

Sample Instructions for First *Group* Peer Response

Read this sheet as soon as you come in; you may need to read it twice; you certainly want to keep it with you to refer to if you forget what to do next.*

More than likely the first peer response will be a little bumpy, but you'll quickly learn the process. Bear with yourself and others today as we practice "grouping" and "responding." In the future, instructions won't be quite so prescriptive, but, to get started, *let's use a particular process that usually works well.* Note: These instructions are intended to help you; if they do not, ask me to come to your table to explain.

> *The process described below is based on one demonstrated in "Student Writing groups," available from The Workshop Corp. (see Section IV, page 25.)*

Remember the "key" to peer response is "response," not "edit," not "evaluate," not criticize rudely or destructively. Just tell the writer what you think is good in the draft and what you don't understand (more specific examples in Steps 9 and 10 below). After everyone responds, the readers help the writer "talk through questions" or "problems" by considering things to do to improve. Remember it is your job to assist the writer get a better draft because the next writing is the one that will get a tentative "grade" from the instructor. Being noncommittal or giving only praise are the least effective things you can do. So your goal is to help the writer see the strengths you see and to point to the areas that are problems for you. At the end you should leave some time to discuss the areas the author points out as problems for her.

Remember the "key" to getting the most help for your own paper is to listen without being defensive. In fact, the best thing you as the author can do is to tape your mouth closed and keep busy taking notes on what respondents say. This is hard at first. However, getting defensive or explaining everything you meant won't accomplish the goal. At the end you should budget time to ask respondents for suggestions, for clarification, or restatements of problems. You may say what you were trying to do and ask for help in more closely accomplishing that for the readers. Then tell your readers, "thanks" and move on to the next paper. *[Trust me, this all gets easier. Also remember, the respondents are only giving their reactions; their ideas may not work for you. It is first and last your paper, so you are not required to follow any reader's advise. However, several readers mentioning the same things might be a good indication of the way many readers will respond. The same thing is true of what I have to say (except possibly on editing in later drafts).]*

Steps:

1. **Move furniture** (quietly)

2. **Three people face each other**

3. **Choose the Chair** by the alphabet method—the person whose first name begins with the letter that comes first (or last) in the alphabet

→

4. **Chair gets things started** quickly and keeps time

5. If you are to use *both* note sheets and group response forms, the **Chair also may designate** who will record the group's summary comments on the peer response form.

6. Along with this instruction sheet, **you will receive a packet of "response" *note* sheets** (pages 27-28) as well as *one group* **response form** (Section III B, Forms one through five). The note sheets are for you to use to jot down things you hear in the papers of the other people in your group; the response form is for *your* respondents to answer specific questions about *your* text.

    On the note sheets, complete as much of the top of the page as I request (this time fill it all out) with your name as "respondent," the date, the number of the essay (one, two, whatever), and the draft (early, preliminary, rough) and some kind of identifying phrase, such as the title or the subject or the name of the assignment. In the space that says, "By," put the name of the person who wrote the paper you are taking notes on; then do a sheet for each writer in your group. (You may do one on yourself if you like.)

    After the first reading, quickly write out your initial response (don't take a lot of time thinking); while the paper is being read the second time, use the columns to jot down words or phrases to remind yourself later of the places in the paper where you had a positive or negative response or a question.

7. **Beginning with the person designated by the Chair,** *the author reads aloud*. This is very hard at first, but it is one of the more important parts of the process. *Read slowly* and clearly but not too loudly; if you can't hear someone, stop him; if you still can't hear, your group may have to move elsewhere.

    When it is your turn to read your paper, try not to apologize for it. Many of us have this driving compulsion to tell our listeners what a rotten piece of writing they are about to hear or read. This public self-humiliation is a ritual some must go through before we can expose our writing to the public eye. As compulsive describers of our own shortcomings, of course, we also recognize anotherself-punishing writer about to burst forth. And we know what these ritualistic statements will most likely be. "This is the worst paper I ever wrote," while pulling madly at his hair, or the crisis variation ("My dog had ten puppies last night and I didn't sleep at all"), or (the one I particularly hate) "I know I can do great papers, but I just couldn't get into this topic." If we can avoid this sort of preliminary exorcism, we'll save a lot of time this term. Let's just agree that every early draft is probably weak and certainly no paper is as good as it can be (or as it will be, if we don't spend all our time berating our writing).

8. At the end of each reading, **take a few minutes to write your overall impression** in the space provided on your note sheet. The author may take this time to do the same thing on her self-evaluation sheet (thus becoming a critic of her own text). What stood out? What was your first reaction? Don't be elaborate—just give a brief sense of the paper overall. Try not to give pronouncements of worth: "That was really good," or "I think that would get a bad grade." Don't tell the author what to do; being prescriptive gives a very different feel to the author than when

→

the reader just tries to give his impressions, the "pictures in your mind," as Peter Elbow calls what we do when we try to recreate what was going on in our head while we were listening. An example of an adequate initial response is something like, "Your topic interests me; I've never had a chance to read that book, and now I really want to. I'm not sure you say enough specific things, though, to support some of your points. I'd like to hear more about why Seth is a victim but is not victimized."

9. After the paper is read once and respondents have written overall impressions, **the paper is read a second time** (the author does not have to read both times; sometimes it helps to hear our words spoken by someone else). Someone reads; you listen and take careful notes; then each respondent, by looking at your overall impression and at your notes, can comment at least on several positive things, several questions, and several problems. For instance, "In the question column, I wrote down the word 'butterfly' because I was thinking, 'Is this the subject?' I thought I'd be getting the main idea by that point, but I wasn't sure." OR "The next word in my question column was 'buzzard,' because I couldn't see how the middle of the paper relates to the first part." OR "I also wrote down 'transgression,' but I don't remember why, just something about that word, but my main question by the end was, 'Do you have a thesis yet?'")

   Or, you don't know whether it's a problem or not, but you might say something like, "That part in the first paragraph about the colors in the story made me see the scene. But somewhere after the words 'balmy,' or maybe it was, 'I'm not sure what the color purple has to do with balmy.' I was thinking about that, you know, and then pretty soon my head was off the paper. I tuned back in where you started talking about the shades of red that 'follow Panna like a road map.' That's about the spot where I came out of my snooze. Probably just my brain going dead, but maybe that's a problem—I mean, you know, like not really keeping the reader tracking with you."

10. When time allows, the author asks for help in those areas he listed on his self-evaluation. The respondents may engage the author in explaining why that area seems troublesome and, rather than offering solutions, ask him questions to help him find solutions. Respondents also may make specific suggestions. "Your theme statement isn't a statement, is it? Shouldn't you say, 'Gordimer is writing a modern-day version of the Garden of Eden' rather than 'Is *The Silent Voice of the Serpent* Gordimer's recreation of the Garden of Eden?'"

   The whole group may have to work on finding out what the paper is trying to say, what its focus is, what its thesis is, perhaps even backtrack to the interpretation of the primary text, looking at where the writer may need more work developing the interpretation. (Early drafts are pesky creatures that don't always have a clear direction.)

11. **Then repeat this process with each paper.** Each respondent will give his note sheet to the author of the paper. Or, said another way, each note sheet should end up attached to the paper the notes are about. The response form itself also goes with the paper. The time to complete the response form is at the end of the comment period, after the author has had a chance to ask ques-

→

tions. The author may review later all of the written comments, those on individual note sheets as well as on the response form. Furthermore, I want to see them with the paper they are a response to so I can evaluate how much you are getting as you listen. (The author can turn all notes and response forms in to me with the second draft of the paper; that way the author keeps the comments for revision purposes if she likes.)

12. **Just try to keep in mind that the respondents' job is to help the writer so he or she will make good grades in the portfolio draft. Therefore, you as author want to get as much from these people as you can: keep what helps or makes sense, forget the rest.**

TYPES OF RESPONDENTS

Identify the following respondent types in a few words. Remember most of us are a combination; problems occur when a respondent acts totally as one of these.

The Boss	The Bored	The Bold
The Cheerleader	The Cynic	The Clown/Jokster/Tease
The Debater	The Expert	The Fidgeter/Distracter
The Defensive	The Invisible	The Know It All
The Monopolizer	The Never Organized	The Always Organized
The Shy One	The Facilitator	The Procrastinator
The Socializer	The Whiner	The Wise One

NOTE SHEET INSTRUCTIONS*

- Each respondent uses a set of note sheets for each paper to which you respond.
- During the first reading, just listen; at the end of the reading, on the top of the note sheet, write a summary sentence about your overall response.
- During the second reading, make notes in the appropriate columns of words or phrases from the paper at the points where you responded favorably (to an idea, a sentence, a way of developing—it doesn't matter—just write down a word to remind yourself later), or had a question, or did not have a positive response (even if you don't know what you responded to negatively). If you try to write more, you will not be able to listen to the text as well.
- At the end of the two readings, each respondent reads her comments. Then the first respondent talks from her note sheet. When it is your turn to speak, you should have quite a bit to say just by reading the list of words in each column. Whether or not you remember why you wrote something down, the author at least knows where to look; often, however, the word will remind you of what you were thinking at that point.
- If a previous respondent has noted the same things, you can say that and only discuss where your response was different or if you have something to add to the previous respondents' comments.

PURPOSES OF NOTE SHEETS:
- to provide the writer with specific commentary
- to avoid having little to say or saying only general things
- to practice taking notes (as opposed to trying to write down everything a speaker says or to write in sentences and phrases)
- to practice concentration skills (most of us are not particularly good listeners)
- to validate to the teacher your participation in the group work

This process is based on the one used in the video, "Student Writing Groups"; however, any number of methods of organizing responses can be effective. In some cases you may only read notes the respondent gives you on the essay itself or you may do all of your reading and writing in response outside of class.

Note Sheets for Peer Response

NAME OF AUTHOR AND TITLE OF PAPER*
_____

ASSIGNMENT NAME OR NUMBER ("ESSAY 1" OR "PAPER ON SHORT STORY")
_____

DRAFT NUMBER OR NAME ("DRAFT 1 OF PAPER 1" OR "EARLY DRAFT OF PAPER 2")
_____

NAME OF RESPONDENT_____

DATE_____

*The idea of making notes in columns labeled as positive, negative, and questions is taken from the video "Student Writing Groups" (see Section IV list of references for more information on access to the tape).

OVERALL COMMENTS OR RESPONSE AFTER FIRST READING: TAKE ONLY ONE OR TWO MINUTES FOR THIS FIRST RESPONSE.		
POSITIVE ☺	PROBLEMS ☹	QUESTIONS ?

→

PEER RESPONSE NOTE SHEET

POSITIVE ☺	PROBLEMS ☹	QUESTIONS ?

Section III. A.

Self-Evaluations

INSTRUCTIONS FOR SELF-EVALUATIONS

(If you want to complete your self-evaluations on your computer, just put your name at the top of the page give the form name and number ("I. A. 1. Self-Evaluation of Early Draft") and then number your responses to correspond to the questions on the form. Follow your instructor's directions about whether you must write in complete sentences or whether you may respond in words and phrases.)

PURPOSES

- to help writers to be more objective about their texts;
- to practice reflection about writing and thinking;
- to help readers assist in improving the paper.

With the latter in mind, be as specific and as focused as possible in your naalysis.

AVOID

- questions that can be answered "yes" or "no" ("Do you like it?");
- general questions ("What can be improved?");
- questions that aren't appropriate for the draft (asking for help on spelling in an early draft).

TRY INSTEAD TO

- ask focused and specific questions ("Is there enough said about the point that Seth does not indulge in self-pity?").

FORM III. A. 1. *(Form "H" in first edition)*

SELF-EVALUATION TO ACCOMPANY ESSAY FOR PEER RESPONSE

In order to help your instructor or peer reader respond to this essay, you should explain where you are in the writing process. Be as specific as possible in answering the following questions.

1. What are you trying to say in this paper? What is your main idea?

2. Who might be interested in reading this paper?

3. What do you like best in the paper?

4. What do you like least in your paper?

5. What would you work on if you had 24 hours more to spend on the project?

6. What three questions would you like to ask your reader? How can your reader help you develop the paper further?

SELF-EVALUATION IN SECOND ROUND OF THOROUGH CRITIQUE

*Thorough Critique: Tori Haring-Smith's original peer evaluation forms used this designation for response sessions consisting of very complete response, including comments on ways to improve the paper and also responses to the author's questions called for below. This is a good basic self-evaluation form for early or revised drafts.

AUTHOR'S NAME:_____

RESPONDENT'S NAME(S):_____

(Author: Please attach a revision of your original paper to this form and answer the following questions.)

1. What do you think is your reader's point of view on this subject? Do you share that point of view?

2. What assumptions does your reader make about the topic?

3. What two comments by the respondents were the most useful? Why were they helpful?

4. What are the two most important changes that you have made in this revision?

5. What do you like best about the essay?

6. What two questions would you like your respondents to answer about this revision?

Self-Evaluation for Early (Discovery) Draft

AUTHOR'S NAME:_____

TENTATIVE TITLE OR SUBJECT OF THIS
DRAFT:_____

1. Quickly jot down a list of things you did to prepare for this assignment including reading instructions, texts, other people's work, other texts, thinking, generating, writing.

2. What did you learn in doing this much of the assignment?

3. Is anything emerging as a center of gravity for you, an area of interest you keep being pulled back to, an image that continues to come to your mind? If so, what? If not, what will you do for the next step of the project?

4. What do you include or cover in the materials you have brought with you today? Is there a focus in this? If so, what? If not, after reading your materials to the group, discuss with them possible centers or patterns that they may see emerging or you may begin to locate just by reading and discussing the work. Write in the space below some possibilities. Even if you had decided on a focus or had a theme or thesis, look at your materials again to see if anything is changing that you want to reexamine and redraft. If so what is that?

5. On a scale of one to five, with five being excellent, how do you rate your work so far:

   • time spent on gathering information, generating ideas   _____

   • quality of the actual materials gathered (usefulness in making you think,
     or in value of information or even possible quality of the writing itself)   _____

→

- time spent on drafting (and revising perhaps)   _____

- quality of reading of texts for ideas   _____

- any original research you have done   _____

- theme or focus developing or potential for developing   _____

- value of risk you have taken in this project   _____

- value of this work in building toward another text   _____

7. On this draft, to what do you want your instructor to respond the most carefully?

Self-Evaluation for Early Draft (Short Form)

(Use the back of page if needed or answer on separate paper.)

Author's Name:_____

1. The greatest strength of my paper at this point is

2. Three of the weakest areas in this draft and/or three specific problems I want respondents to address are

   A.

   B.

   C.

3. Based on the criteria we established for writing in the genre into which this paper could fall (personal essay, critical interpretation, news report, persuasive essay with documentation, etc.) and considering that this is an early draft, I think the draft is

_____ Good, as it is; needs these things (fill in space provided under question 6 below):

_____ Pretty good for an early draft; needs these things:

_____ Poor, even for an early draft; I plan to try these things:

_____ Weak, even for an early draft; I plan to do these things:

4. I have made a major investment of time and energy in this draft so far. Yes____ No____

5. Check the sentence that applies:

_____ I am moderately committed to this topic.

_____ I am extremely committed to this topic.

_____ I really am not too interested in this topic.

OR the part of the topic that interests me the most after doing this draft is

6. Based on my readers' comments and my analysis in question 3, I plan the following:

Self-Evaluation for Revised Draft of Out-of-Class Essay

Author's Name:_____

Title of Paper:_____

1. At this stage the primary audience for this paper is

2. Their overall interest in or attitude toward this topic probably is

3. Their overall knowledge on the topic is

4. The areas with which they might disagree include

5. Specific things I've done to address the audience in terms of my responses to questions 2, 3, 4 include (list at least three)

6. Eventually, I hope to make this paper good enough to submit to the_____essay contest to be judged by_____.

7. I've given particular considerations to the following areas for success with that audience.

8. Two of the major revisions in this draft from the one my respondents saw last include

9. Check below if the statement applies.

    I have made significant improvements in these areas of the form of my paper:

    theme statement (if writing a literary analysis)   _____

    thesis statement   _____

    overall organization   _____

    development   _____

    polished sentences and syntax   _____

    mechanical aspects of the paper (punctuation, spelling, grammar)   _____

10. I also have made improvements in the following areas of content:

    sophistication of argument   _____

→

depth of analysis   _____

connections and relationships between and among stories (if applicable)   _____

11. I still need help from my group as I plan to work on the following:

12. Using a 5 to indicate "excellent"; 4 to indicate "good"; 3 for "fair"; 2 for "weak"; and 1 for "needy"; I evaluate the paper in the following areas as indicated by the number shown.

overall it addresses the audience in an interesting way   Number_____

clearly states a position and supports that position   Number_____

uses evidence from the text   Number_____

includes careful and thorough analysis and accurate information Number_____

is thought provoking   Number_____

well-organized   Number_____

well-developed   Number_____

edited for syntax and diction   Number_____

includes necessary documentation in correct form   Number_____

13. After the peer response, if I were to work more on this paper, I would do the following:

14. I would like for the instructor to answer the following questions and/or pay particular attention to the areas of the paper indicated below.

Self-Evaluation for Publication (or Final) Draft

(You may use the back if needed.)

Author's Name:_____

1. What are two things you think are good about this draft?

2. What do you think the greatest weakness is?

3. If you had more time to revise, what would you do?

4. What are two important things you learned, or improved, about writing while working on this assignment?

5. What are two (or more) specific things you tried for the first time or you practiced doing, knowing you might not do them well? In other words, tell me the exact places or the exact things you did to take a risk with this writing (I reward risk, even if it's not successful, so be specific here).

6. What techniques or effective strategies did you use in this paper that you plan to continue in future papers?

7. What aspects of this draft would you most like the instructor to respond to or do you prefer a grade only?

SELF-EVALUATION FOR REVISED DRAFT SHORT FORM

AUTHOR'S NAME_____

1. I have "re-seen" and revised my earlier draft in these major ways.

2. Specifically, I have made these revisions (name the paragraph and page) *OR* This is only an editing of the previous draft. The reason is that

3. The major strengths of this paper now are

4. The major problems are

5. The major investment I've made in this draft is in

6. If I had more time, or if I use this paper in my portfolio, I will do these things:

Self-Evaluation for Materials in Portfolio

(You may answer on separate paper; just number your responses.)

1. Briefly describe the process by which this piece (these pieces) developed. Did you have some sudden insight you decided to pursue? Did some particular point or issue or question intrigue you to find an answer or to understand a concept? Did you just finally give up and go back to some previous essays to revise? Most important, in answering this question, please record why you chose this particular piece (these pieces) for the major project or for the portfolio submission.

2. What are three particular aspects of the writing in this piece that you think are good or work well?

3. What is one area you think is not as strong? If you had more time, what would you do to improve this area?

4. How do you envision the audience, purpose, and possible place(s) of publication for the writing(s)? Point to several moments in the text(s) in which you were consciously considering your audience(s) and purpose(s).

5. In what ways did you take risks in developing this text? Point specifically to areas of risk in the formulation of ideas, in the topic, in the approach, in certain writing strategies within the essay or the drafts and other writings leading up to the portfolio draft. What, if any, payoff was there for the writing, or for you as a writer, by taking that risk?

6. What specific things did you learn about reading in writing this essay? About writing in general in the process of writing this essay? About writing specifically in this essay? What techniques for discovering ideas, adjusting ideas, developing ideas did you learn in the process of the overall development of this product in its present form? What did you learn about using authorities? What did you learn about developing your own points and ideas? What did you learn about doing and using library research? In what, if any, ways do you think you will continue in future classes or in your career to use some of the things you learned?

7. What roles did your group's reading of your papers and your reading of theirs and the discussions in response to your texts and the professional texts play in (a) your development of your ideas; (b) your understanding of concepts from the "experts"; (c) the form or the means by which you conveyed your understanding and your knowledge in the portfolio product? How likely are you to continue to use a reading/learning/writing group in the future?

8. Can you now discuss what constitutes "good writing" and evaluate how good your writing in

→

this piece is based on that criteria? If yes, do so. If not, write out the comment you would make on your paper if the paper were written by someone you don't know. Also include the letter grade you would give the paper and why.

9. On a scale of one to five, with five being excellent, how would you rank the depth of your knowledge on the topic of your essay(s)? On your original thinking on the topic? On your sense of yourself as an "expert" on the topic, someone who could engage in dialogue with other "knowledgeable peers."

10. If appropriate, please comment on how the work for this portfolio or with the major project(s) has changed, expanded, or revised your ideas about reading, writing, pursuing knowledge.

FORMS FOR PEER RESPONSE EARLY DRAFTS

SHORT INSTRUCTIONS FOR COMPLETING PEER RESPONSE FORMS

PURPOSES

- of peer response are to help the writer improve the text

- by pointing out possible problems that block access to meaning

- and by giving the author a sense of readers' responses to subject, argument, or even a way of expressing points.

DO

- Follow instructor's directions as to whether each respondent writes out answers to the questions OR if one respondent records the common responses among readers, noting any differences by initials of the respondent.

- Attach sheet(s) to the paper they describe.

- Be as specific as possible. (Avoid judgments and generalizations.).

- Point to specific places in the text by paragraph number or sentence if possible.

- Respond to those areas most applicable for the stage the paper is in (i.e., comment on overall organization, development of arguments on early drafts; save stylistic comments and editing for later drafts).

- Use language that discusses the "paper" (i.e., "In the first sentence of paragraph two, the paper to me is arguing the opposite of what I think the point of the paper is").

DON'T

- Appropriate the paper. Remember it belongs to the writer who ultimately will decide what to do on the next draft.

- Say little or nothing.

- Make comments in terms of the writer ("You should have done this").

READER RESPONSE SHEET FOR DESCRIPTIVE CRITIQUE*

*In a descriptive critique, the reader responds simply by telling the author what the reader believes the paper is about, without any response as to the effect of the form or content of the paper on the reader. Therefore, it also is a "short" response.

AUTHOR'S NAME:_____

RESPONDENT'S NAME(S):_____

1. Read the first paragraph and then pause. Write down what you expect the topic, purpose, and audience of the paper will be.

2. Now finish reading the paper. Were your expectations for the paper's topic, purpose, and audience fulfilled? If not, what do you now think the topic, purpose, and audience are?

4. What sort of evidence is used to develop or support this main idea?

5. Summarize the paper, devoting one sentence to each paragraph.

READER RESPONSE FOR EVALUATIVE CRITIQUE*

*In the evaluative critique, the reader tells what the paper is about and also analyzes the paper's strengths and weaknesses.

AUTHOR'S NAME_____

RESPONDENT'S NAME(S)_____

1. Read the first paragraph and then pause. Write down what you expect the topic, purpose, and audience of the paper will be.

2. Now finish reading the paper. Were your expectations for the paper's topic, purpose, and audience fulfilled? If not, what do you now think the topic, purpose, and audience are?

3. What do you think the main idea or thesis of the paper is?

4. What sort of evidence is used to develop or support this main idea?

5. Summarize the paper, devoting one sentence to each paragraph.

6. What did you like best about the paper?

→

7. Did anything in the paper surprise you?

8. What two features of the paper most need improvement?

9. Please respond to the author's questions (below).
   [**To the author:** Before giving this sheet to your reader, list the three questions that you would like your reader to answer about this paper.]

   1.

   2.

   3.

Reader Response for Thorough Critique*

*Thorough critique describes the paper, comments on strengths and weaknesses and, more specifically than Forms 1 and 2, analyzes the paper's arguments; therefore, this form is appropriate for an expository/argumentative essay.

AUTHOR'S NAME:_____

RESPONDENT'S NAME(S):_____

If the author has included a self-evaluation, do not read it until you have answered questions 1 through 3.

1. Read the first paragraph and then pause. Write down what you expect the topic, purpose, and audience of the paper will be.

2. Now finish reading the paper. Were your expectations for the paper's topic, purpose, and audience fulfilled? If not, what do you now think the topic, purpose, and audience are?

3. Summarize the paper, devoting one sentence to each paragraph.

4. What do you think the main idea or thesis of the paper is? Do you agree with this thesis? Why or why not? What is your position on this topic?

5. What sort of evidence is used to develop or support this main idea? Is this evidence appropriate? Is there sufficient evidence? If not, what sort of evidence should the writer consider?

→

6. Does the author take into account different points of view about the thesis of the paper? Does the author consider counter arguments?

7. Are there any counter arguments that the author does not consider, but should?

8. What did you like best about this paper?

9. What two features of the paper most need improvement?

10. Please respond to the author's questions below..
[**To the author:** Before giving this sheet to your reader, list below the three questions that you would like your reader to answer about this paper.]

   1.

   2.

   3.

VARIATION ON INSTRUCTIONS FOR PEER RESPONSE BASED ON GROUP METHOD

PEER RESPONSE OVERALL INSTRUCTIONS:

(These instructions follow the format of the response process in the film, *Student Writing Groups*. However, we will vary the procedures described below depending on several factors.)

GETTING STARTED

The first and most important thing is to get to class as early as possible, get with the group you worked with last, or arrange chairs for a group of three, sit down, get out your papers, including your completed self-evaluation, and get settled. As soon as two others have joined you, start to work. As a respondent you should have your response note sheets ready, one for each paper in your group, and one group response form for your partners to fill out when they discuss your paper.

As polite people, we certainly want to greet one another, preferably by name, and engage in other social noises that make us human; even so, let's do get down to business quickly. Time is a factor. So, let's avoid the nitty-gritty of the math test, or the parking problem, or the lines at the financial aid office, or, most especially, the excuses about what you have and haven't done on this assignment. Try to get on task and stay there until either break (if this is a longer time-frame) or the end of class (for the regular fifty-minute sessions).

FIRST READER

The first reader, who immediately volunteered when two respondents were in the group (yeah, I'm only moderately deluded most of the time), reads the entire draft *very slowly and very clearly.* I know at first we just want to hurry up and get this over with, but your listeners will not hear you well if you go fast; you should know how hard this is when you are the respondent trying to listen and take notes. To make it easier for the respondent to follow, do not talk with your head tucked under your shirt, or your pencil, gum, or chew in your mouth, or in a whisper, or in a roar either, or dropping off the endings of words and sentences.

RESPONDENTS

During the first reading respondents just listen, and when the author finishes, write your overall impression of the paper in the space provided on the "Peer Response Note Sheet" (II. C. page 29).

SECOND READING

On the second reading, take *notes.* Do not try to write out complete comments; simply jot down words and phrases *as the paper is read* to remind yourself of places you had questions, other places you thought were good or thought needed work.

→

RESPONDENTS GIVE OVERALL IMPRESSION

After two readings, each respondent reads his or her overall impression aloud to the whole group.

THEN EACH RESPONDENT GIVES COMMENTS FROM NOTES

Next, each of you who is acting as a respondent reads through your notes aloud, commenting on what you remember about your thinking when you wrote the words or phrases from that part of the paper. Sometimes, if you can't remember, the author can reread that sentence or section, which will prompt your recall.

CONSTRUCTIVE CRITICISM

Remember, all criticism, positive and negative, should be couched in terms of the paper, not the person. "The paper seems to be saying this, but in the next paragraph it begins to talk about something else," rather than "You seem to be saying this, but then you shift to. . . ." or "This is right" (good, wrong anything that is evaluative). You are not an expert in right and wrong but you are an expert in what strikes you as effective, not so effective, etc. "The way I hear this is. . . ." OR "That works for me (or does not work for me)." "What would happen if you. . . ?" "Could you just say to me what this says to you?" Questions generally are more acceptable than commands, "You should have said. . . ." or "Move that paragraph. . . ." On the other hand, saying, "I like it," or "That's good." or "Good essay—just needs a little. . . ." is not any help and should be insulting and unacceptable to the author and always is unacceptable to me. After all respondents have commented as fully as possible, go on to the next paper.

AUTHOR'S PROCESS

Before reading your paper, do not make apologies for it. We will just assume that no one's paper is too wonderful, and rather than waste time with comments like, "I really didn't have time to work on this" or "I don't usually write this bad" or "I just hate this topic," or one of my least favorite, "Well, I really didn't understand what we were supposed to do." All of this is just warm-up noise, which is possibly okay if we have lots of time, but we don't. So just read. While respondents are commenting, the author LISTENS and takes notes. Don't defend your paper or ask questions. Don't be hostile or antagonistic about the comments, because even the most poorly stated criticism may be of help, which, after you are familiar with the process, is much better than no criticism, or criticism that doesn't offer any constructive comments about revision. "It's really good," is nice to hear, but if it isn't followed with more substantive remarks, all of you have wasted your time.

After all respondents have finished, the author may explain, ask for suggestions, or request responses to the areas you thought were weak when you read it or heard it. You certainly should ask for comments on the areas you indicated as weaknesses on your self-evaluation. Do not settle for less than a full hearing and a full response. I expect you to evaluate your respondents accordingly, as they will you when you respond. And always think, "Am I doing my best to help my partners get

→

as high an evaluation as possible, as well as to write the best essay possible for the audience and the purpose and in the time we have for the assignment?"

GROUP EVALUATION RESONSE FORM ON THESIS, TOPIC, ETC.

If the group has time at the end, one person should fill out the group comments on questions attached to this sheet. This does not mean one person answers the questions; it means the group discusses the possible answers and the recorder fills in the form.

WHAT TO DO WITH THE PAPERS

The individual note sheets must be placed with the paper, so each paper has as many note sheets as there are respondents in the group; in addition, it has one response form completed for that paper. (Remember, I want to check how well you are doing as respondents; naturally, I need the response form and the note sheets with the paper.)

✏

READER RESPONSE BY GROUP FOR EARLY DRAFT

Peer response pages should be completed by the group after you have given your comments from your notes to the author. One person should act as recorder for the respondents after discussing the answers to the questions below. The author should refrain from providing the answers unless the respondents cannot do so after a reasonable time. If the answers do not correspond to the author's intent and the group has time, the author may ask for suggestions on bringing the next draft more in line with the writer's intent.

AUTHOR'S NAME:_____

RESPONDENTS' NAMES:_____

Title of paper or some designation: "Draft one of Interview paper or Revision of First out-of-class essay"

Is this an early draft?_____   Or   Is this a revised draft?_____

1. What do you think is the thesis or the main idea of the paper? Write it out.

2. What do you think are the topic sentences of the paragraphs?

3. Do the sentences hang together (can they be read as a coherent paragraph)? If not, what did you suggest to the author?

4. How long is the paragraph? What is one specific detail in each body paragraph? If paragraphs needed more development, what did you suggest?

IF YOU HAVE TIME, ANSWER THE FOLLOWING QUESTIONS AS WELL:

5. What are some of the strengths and weaknesses of the paper?

→

SHORT RESPONSE FORM FOR EARLY (DISCOVERY) DRAFTS

AUTHOR'S NAME_____

RESPONDENTS' NAMES: _____

Recorder should describe below the methods you used to hear, see, respond to the materials. (This should include questions you helped the author generate to get more materials for the next draft, summary of the discussion and the suggestions, and the group's perception of where this paper might go from here.)

Section III. B. 2.

Forms for Peer Response Revised Drafts

RESPONSE SHEETS FOR SECOND ROUND OF THOROUGH CRITIQUE

AUTHOR'S NAME_____

RESPONDENT(S) NAME(S)_____

[Author: Please attach a revision of your original paper to this form.]

1. Summarize the author's revision, devoting one sentence to each paragraph.

2. How do you think the author has improved the essay?

3. Has the author changed your feeling about the topic?

4. What is the strongest counterargument to the positions expressed in the revised essay?

5. What two features most need improvement?

6. Respond to the author's questions.

RESPONSE SHEETS FOR REVISED DRAFTS

SECTION III. B. 2. FORM 2.

Complete this form after going through the notes on your note sheets. One respondent should record the group's response, but the group is responsible for the contents, so check over the form before putting it, along with all respondents' note sheets, with a copy of the early draft and the revision of the paper to which the responses apply.

AUTHOR'S NAME:_____

RESPONDENTS' NAMES_____

Paper Number _____Draft Number_____Title of Paper_____

1. We believe the thesis of this paper is stated in _____ (give the exact location). The thesis is

2. The major revisions in this paper from the previous draft include the following:

3. According to the criteria established for letter grades, the areas that still need work to be an acceptable paper (C level) are these

4. The areas that need more work if the paper is to earn a "B" are these

5. The areas that need more work if the paper is to earn an "A" are the following

6. The thing(s) we like the most about this draft of this paper is (are)

7. The responses we made to the author's questions include

RESPONSE SHEETS FOR REVISED DRAFTS/SHORT FORM

(Note to author. Attach both the original paper and the revision to this form. Also attach all of your respondents' note sheets, as well as this summary sheet.)

AUTHOR'S NAME:_____

RESPONDENTS' NAMES:_____

1. Summarize the major comments, suggestions for the next draft, replies to the author's questions.

2. Be certain to include the things you note the author has done to improve the essay.

3. Be certain also to mention the genre or form of the essay and to comment on the particular aspects of that form the author has paid attention to (i.e., if this is a letter to the editor of a campus newspaper, is the tone appropriate to the audience and the writer's purpose OR if this is a feature article on a person, what has been included that makes the person "come alive" for the reader?).

RESPONSE SHEETS FOR MISCELLANEOUS GENRES, AUDIENCES, PURPOSES

Response Sheets for Miscellaneous Genres, Audiences, Purposes Descriptive/Narrative Essay

Author's Name_____

Respondents' Names:_____

1. What about this essay makes you think it should be evaluated on the effectiveness of its narrative and descriptive technique? (What about the essay makes it seem more of a story than an essay written primarily to inform or to persuade?)

2. What is the story about? What is the point of the story?

3. What techniques of description does the author use particularly well? (Identify these places by paragraph and page number.)

4. Which language is most imagistic? Mark these words, phrases, sentences in the texts with a check mark. What images does that language help you to see, feel, taste, etc.

5. Which sections of the essay contain the story line, the things that happen? Are those actions in a logical sequence (this does not necessarily mean a chonological sequence). What is the sequence?

6. Is there any dialogue? Does it sound real, convincing? Is it set up and punctuated correctly? Indicate by page and paragraph where that dialogue is.

→

7. Does the writing get your attention immediately? Why? If not, what do you suggest?

8. Does it keep your attention? If yes, why? If not, where did you lose interest? What do you suggest?

9. What do you think is the author's purpose and how well is that accomplished?

10. What is the title? Does it help the reader understand the story? Can you suggest other good titles?

11. What group(s) would be a good audience for this story? Can you name any specific places it could be published?

12. What suggestions for improvement in any areas do you have?

13. How did you answer the author's questions?

RESPONSE SHEETS FOR PAPER WITH DOCUMENTATION

AUTHOR'S NAME:_____

RESPONDENTS' NAMES:_____

1. What is the thesis of the paper?

2. Where is it stated?

3. A. If the paper is an argument, then who does the author want to convince of what? Does the author take into account what these readers know about the topic? How and where? If not, what do you suggest?

   B. Does the author take into account the probable positions on the argument that the audience may have? How? Where? If not, why not? Do you agree with the author's position? If not, why not? Even if you do agree with the author's position, what are some counter-arguments to the author's position? Does the paper try to address any of those arguments? If so, how? If not, what do you suggest?

4. Is the evidence provided convincing? Is it sufficient, considering the audience? What kind of evidence is included besides authority?

5. Is the argument arranged in a logical sequence? If not, what do you suggest?

6. Does the argument make any effort to appeal to readers' emotions? What appeals are employed? How well do those strategies work? Can you suggest others?

→

7. Look at the works cited page. List the kinds of sources used. What are they? Is there variety? What are the dates? Do the sources seem current for the topic? Are the sources by people you recognize as authorities? If not, does the author provide any annotation of the references or any explanations within the text about whom these people are and why he might be citing them?

9. Are the sources arranged on the page correctly according to MLA format? If not, what is wrong?

10. Are the source entries punctuated correctly? Do not correct any errors but put a queston mark in front of the entry so the author can double check those you question?

11. Read through the text again,paying attention to quotations and paraphrases. Does the author introduce paraphrases in a way to make it clear where they begin and end? If so, where? If not, mark places in the text the author should revise.

12. Is the in-text citation set up and punctuated correctly? Mark any you think are wrong but do not correct them.

13. Does the paper seem to balance the use of authorities with other types of evidence, for instance, personal experiences, primary research, such as interviews or surveys? If not, discuss with the author ways to make the text less reliant on library sources.

14. What are the areas the author should work on most for the next draft? Place a check by the ones that apply. List any others you note that need review but are not included on the following list.
Format
Punctuation
Spacing
Quality of Sources
Balance of types of sources
Balance of quotations, paraphrase, author's own ideas, opinions, and original research
Others (Name)

→

15. A. If this is an early draft, on a scale of one to five, with five being excellent, how do you rate the paper?

   B. If this is a revised draft, what has been changed? How much is the text improved by the revisions? On a scale of one to five, again with five as excellent, how would you rate this draft?

   C. How close to being ready for the portfolio do you rate the draft? (Circle the one that best applies):

   ready now; almost there; still needs major work on (check any that are appropriate)

   style, documentation, research (primary and/or secondary), organization, persuasive elements, format, editing, other (name other).

Response Form for a Literary Analysis (Any Draft)

(Note: only one peer response per paper; *this response sheet itself goes with the paper.*) Work quickly on the paper work and do not spend all of your time trying to write. One person should write and everyone should talk to the author. Asking the author questions is fine. Do not tell the author he is "wrong," or, "This is or isn't good." Rather, point to the specific places you have questions or suggestions. Work from the notes you took as you listened to the paper being read.

AUTHOR'S NAME:_____

RESPONDENTS' NAMES:_____

1. The things we like best about this paper at this point are

2. The main thesis of the paper at this point seems to be

   or

   or

3. What does the author present as the theme(s) of the stories examined? Where are those themes stated, or are they implied? How are the theme statements different from the author's thesis statement, or is the thesis implied?

4. The audience for the paper seems to be, or could be,

→   83

5. The paper gives that audience enough information about the literature discussed based on how familiar they are with the text(s) and based on the positions or views they might hold about the literature. If yes, point to specific paragraphs and sentences. If not, suggest what could be revised.

6. What kinds of evidence does the author use (direct quotations from the text, brief examples of events, personal experience)? Is the evidence enough and strong enough to be convincing to an audience who is not too familiar with this story?
To someone who has at least read the story?
To other critics who know the work well?

7. Does the author sound familiar with the text or as if she is writing about texts she understands? Can you point to places that demonstrate her involvement with the texts and/or with her arguments? If not, can you suggest what needs to be done for the author to sound authoritative and/or more involved in the points she is arguing?

8. What needs to be done to improve the overall organization and coherence?

9. What are at least two ways to make the paper more interesting?

RESPONSE FORMS FOR INTERVIEW ARTICLE (OR FEATURE ARTICLE FOR A MAGAZINE OR NEWSPAPER)

AUTHOR'S NAME_____

YOUR NAME_____

(For this response, you are working either with the person you interviewed only or with another team of two people who interviewed one another. As the person about whom the article is written it is appropriate to comment on the accuracy of the information and indicate to the author if there is anything you would prefer to have omitted or that needs to be changed. In fact, it is most important that you do tell the author if any of the text makes you uncomfortable, since this document will be published for the class.)

1. Does the author follow the instructions for format, length, placement of name, etc. If not, what needs to be redone?

2. Is the information organized? If not, what do you suggest?

3. Does the title indicate the focus of the article? Is the title interesting? If not, work together to come up with some other possible titles. Does the opening sentence get your attention (or do you think it will get the attention of your classmates when they see this article in the Interview Book)? Suggestions?

4. Answer the following questions about the content. Whenever appropriate, make some suggestions for possible changes.

   A. Is the information accurate?

   B. Is the information complete enough?

   C. Does the author quote you and, if so, are the quotations accurate?

→

D. Is the information more than an "all-points-bulletin"? For instance, do you think it conveys the "you" you would like to have presented to the class? What specifically is in the text that makes you the unique person you are (or is the material too "generic" to give a real sense of your personality)?

E. Is there anything the author doesn't include you would like to have included?

F. Is there any material you want to have omitted?

5. Indicate places where the language is particularly concrete, specific, imagistic or sensory.

6. Do all of the sentences seem coherent? Are they varied in structure and length? If not, what can you suggest?

7. How much editing does this draft need? Put a check mark by any places you think may be usage, grammatical, or punctuation errors.

8. Overall, what can you suggest to improve the draft?

RESPONSE FORMS FOR ASSIGNMENT STRESSING PARAGRAPHING

AUTHOR'S NAME_____

RESPONDENTS' NAMES_____

If the author has included a self-evaluation, do not read it until you have answered questions 1 through 6.

1. Read the first paragraph and then pause. Write down what you expect the topic, purpose, and audience of the paper will be.

2. Now finish reading the paper. Were your expectations for the paper's topic, purpose, and audience fulfilled? If not, what do you now think the topic, purpose, and audience are?

3. What do you think the main idea or thesis of the paper is?

4. What sort of evidence is used to develop or support this main idea?

5. First, number the paragraphs. Are the author's paragraphs unified, coherent and developed? If so, note them by number below. Also indicate any that confuse you, and explain why.

6. Do the paragraphs follow a logical order? List each pair of neighboring paragraphs and describe how the argument does or does not flow from the first to the second.

→

7. What did you like best about the paper?

8. What two features of the paper most need improvement?

RESPONSE FORM FOR AN ESSAY ASSIGNMENT STRESSING CLEAR AND EFFECTIVE SNTENCES

(Note: If the author has included a self-evaluation, do not read it until you have answered questions 1 through 4.)

AUTHOR'S NAME:_____

RESPONDENTS' NAMES:_____

1. Read the first paragraph and then pause. Write down what you expect the topic, purpose, and audience of the paper will be.

2. Now finish reading the paper. Were your expectations for the paper's topic, purpose, and audience fulfilled? If not, what do you now think the topic, purpose and audience are?

3. What do you think the main idea or the thesis of the paper is?

4. What kinds of evidence does the author use to develop or support the main idea?

5. Were the author's sentences easy to read? Number the paragraphs and sentences and indicate below any that you thought were confusing. Next to the sentence numbers, try to explain why the sentences were confusing.

Paragraph   Sentence Number   Problem

→

6. Did you notice any grammatical problems in the author's sentences? If so, list below the paragraph number, sentence number and the grammatical problem.

    Paragraph   Sentence Number   Problem

7. Describe the most common sentence structure found in the author's paper. Does the author vary sentence structure? If so, describe two instances in which sentence variety was especially effective. If not, suggest places where sentences need to be more varied.

8. What did you like best about the paper?

9. What are the two features of the paper that most need improvement?

GRID FOR QUICK PEER RESPONSE EARLY AND REVISED DRAFTS

Date_____   Name_____
Assessing Writing   Class Period_____

strong		okay		weak		FEATURES OF DRAFT/FINAL
						INTRODUCTION: establishes idea, sets context, orients and engages the reader
						CONTENTS: insights, thinking, grappling with topic
						FOCUS/CLARITY: key ideas are sufficiently clear; thesis is clear and well-stated
						DEVELOPMENT: ideas are well-developed and supported by appropriate stories, examples and/or references to the readings
						ORGANIZATION: structure, transitions; logical arrangement of ideas
						COMPLETENESS: adequately covers the topic and/or the assignment
						VOICE/STYLE: energy, personality, presence; active verbs
						REVISION: reworking, rethinking, not just editing
						INVESTMENT: evidence of effort, evidence of intellectual energy
						OVERALL IMPRESSION

COMMENTS:

strong		okay		weak		FEATURES OF FINAL
						LANGUAGE: diction/syntax, word choice, phrasing, arrangement
						VERBS:
						PRONOUN REFERENCE:
						EDITING/PROOFREADING
						MECHANICS: capitalization, punctuation
						SPELLING:
						COMMAS:
						APOSTROPHES:
						INVESTMENT: evidence of revision, evidence of effort
						OVERALL IMPRESSION

COMMENTS:

The grid was devised by **Pat Fox,** Director of the Coastal Georgia Writing Project, from materials on criteria for evaluation developed by **Peter Elbow.** She suggests instructors tailor the form to the individual assignments. We appreciate permission to use this sample here.

RESPONSE FORMS APPROPRIATE FOR THE VISUAL LEARNER—"SHOWING THE BIG PICTURE"

The idea for "the big picture" comes from Peter Elbow's *Writing Without Teachers*. His discussions of making "movies of our minds" or describing to authors what readers "see" as we listen to texts, as well as his suggestions about describing a text metaphorically, are the origin of the idea of asking respondents to draw what we hear.

Some of us can draw images of things we see as we listen to a reading, even when we can't draw pictures that anyone else could recognize. Often we "doodle" when we are listening and, while the "doodles" may seem to have nothing to do with what is being said or read, with just a little thought, we can sometimes capture how a text makes us feel by an object that represents our emotions or feelings. Then we can simply tell the author that this is how the text made us respond by showing our picture or describing the feeling.

Peter Elbow also suggests that we imagine the text as something it is not. For instance, if the text were an animal, what animal would it be? Or, if the text were terrain, would it be a mountain or a valley or a field? Visual learners may prefer to draw their metaphoric response.

For instance, your group might decide to describe a text by comparing it to seasons of the year. If you were drawing the picture of a text that is about an event and the episode makes you feel cool and nostalgic, you might draw an image of a person (even a stick figure) reclining by a lake surrounded by tall trees. Or, if we were thinking about our response to a text in terms of architecture, we might draw a gingerbread house with lots of icing and candy windows and doors for an essay that is loaded with details and specific examples. This would be appropriate for a text that is "rich" in its language or complex in its argument. We might draw a very "modern" structure with simple classic lines to indicate clarity and grace or even sophistication of thought. It doesn't really matter what we draw or why; the image may help us to talk about what the text evokes for us.

We can even draw the form of an essay using simple geometrical shapes. Is the organization like a pyramid or an inverted pyramid or the old-fashioned "keyhole" of the five-paragraph essay described by well-known teacher and writer, Sheridan Baker?

In this exercise of giving the movies of our mind, we might think of a screenwriter's "story board" and jot down various "frames" as we listen to a text. Instead of talking from our notes of words and phrases, we can talk from our "story board" or from our series of "doodles" or from the pictures of our metaphors.

Any of these things can be done without the pictures, of course, but for those who "see" things in images, roughly sketching out some of those may help us talk about someone's paper in ways that are different and perhaps more revealing than the usual response to specific questions.

→

At least this can be a variation on the response methods for those times when we are tired of the usual methods, when we just want to be more playful, or when we have a text that doesn't seem to fit other response scenarios.

Try it; you'll probably at least have some fun, especially if you can't draw worth a hoot.

→

Forms for Evaluation of Self, Group, and Individuals as Respondents

SELF-EVALUATION OF PERFORMANCE AS A RESPONDENT

YOUR NAME _____

On a scale of 1-5, rate your performance in the following areas of response effectiveness (5 is extremely well done, 4 is well done, 3 is satisfactory, 2 is weak, and 1 is unsatisfactory—*please provide rationale for a 5 or a 1 on the back by item number*). Consider your overall responses to all papers you've worked on.

1. Listened to papers attentively _____

2. Read papers carefully (if hard copy of text provided) _____

3. Responded Thoroughly _____

4. Diplomatically _____

5. Helpfully critical _____

6. Also asked questions to help writers rethink the text _____

7. Made specific suggestions that might improve the next draft _____

List three ways you were particularly helpful:

Suggestions to be a more helpful respondent:

EVALUATION OF INDIVIDUAL MEMBER OF RESPONSE GROUP

(You do not need to include your own name; the name in the space below is for one of your respondents. You should complete one form on each student you've worked with so far in a peer response group.)

RESPONDENT'S NAME_____

On a scale of 1-5, please rate the respondent, whose name is above, in the following areas of response effectiveness (5 is extremely well done, 4 is well done, 3 is satisfactory, 2 is weak, and 1 is unsatisfactory—*please provide rationale for a 5 or a 1 on the back by item number*). You should consider his/her response to all of the papers in the group, not just your own, and to both drafts of those papers (we all have "off" days).

1. Listened to papers attentively   _____

2. Read papers carefully (if hard copy of text provided)   _____

3. Responded Thoroughly   _____

4. Diplomatically   _____

5. Helpfully critical   _____

6. Also asked questions to help writers rethink the text   _____

7. Made specific suggestions that might improve
the next draft   _____

Comments about ways this respondent was particularly helpful:

Suggestions about how this respondent might be more helpful:

EVALUATION BY INDIVIDUAL MEMBER OF RESPONSE GROUP

YOUR NAME:_____

	Other Group Members:	Specific Assignment (if Applicable)
1.	_____	_____
2.	_____	_____
3.	_____	_____
4.	_____	_____

On a scale of 1 to 5, with one being needs major improvement, moving through fair, good, very good, superior, how do you rate the effectiveness of your group: If you give a 1 or a 5, please comment as to why or give a specific example. Use the back if needed.

	1	2	3	4	5
1. Effectiveness of group in process					
Organized	❏	❏	❏	❏	❏
Efficient (Used time wisely)	❏	❏	❏	❏	❏
Shared responsbilities	❏	❏	❏	❏	❏
Assumed different roles	❏	❏	❏	❏	❏
Worked well in getting peer response forms completed	❏	❏	❏	❏	❏
Avoided one or two people saying too much	❏	❏	❏	❏	❏
Avoided one or two people saying too little	❏	❏	❏	❏	❏

2. Effectiveness of group members in the following areas ilf the group average is lower because of one individual, please note that in the space on the next page for "comments"; you also may note that person by initials, although it is not required to identify by name).

	1	2	3	4	5
Being present	❏	❏	❏	❏	❏
Being on time and staying the whole time	❏	❏	❏	❏	❏
Having materials organized	❏	❏	❏	❏	❏
Volunteering to read first or to be Chair	❏	❏	❏	❏	❏
Giving thorough critiques	❏	❏	❏	❏	❏
Keeping critiques diplomatic	❏	❏	❏	❏	❏
Helping each other ask good questions	❏	❏	❏	❏	❏
Maintaining a good attitude	❏	❏	❏	❏	❏

→

3. What is this group's greatest strength?

4. What is the area that this group most needs to improve?

5. Overall, and excluding yourself, in your group, who contributed the most of substance to the discussions and to the group processes?

6. If you could work with only one member of the group again, who would that be and why?

7. If you could, would you stay with this group as it is? OR Would you rather work with another group?

8. Comments:

Section IV. Additional Resources

ADDITIONAL RESOURCES RELATED TO PEER RESPONSE

> **ABBREVIATIONS**
> CCC—College Composition and Communication
> CE—College English
> EJ—English Journal
> MLA—The Modern Language Association of America
> NCTE—National Council of Teachers of English
> RTE—Research in the Teaching of Writing

Abercombie, M. L. J. *Talking to Learn: Improving Teaching and Learning in Small Groups.* Soc. For Research in Higher Education. Surrey: U. Of Surrey, 1978.

Aik, Kam Chaun, and Stephen Edmonds. *Critical Thinking: Selected Topics for Discussions and Analysis.* Singapore: Longman, 1976.

Anson, Chris M. *Writing and Response.* Urbana, Il: NCTE, 1989.

Applebee, Arthur N. *Tradition and Reform in the Teaching of English: A History.* Urbana, IL: NCTE, 1974.

Beaven, Mary H. "Individualized Goal Setting, Self-Evaluation, and Peer Evaluation." Cooper and Odell, *Evaluating,* 135–136.

Beginning Writing Groups. Produced by Wordshop Productions. 1991. Videocassette.*

Berlin, James. "Contemporary Composition: The Major Pedagogical Theories." *CE* 44 (Dec. 1982): 765–77.

Berliner, David and Ursula Casanova. "Peer Tutoring: A New Look at a Popular Practice." *Instructor* 97(1988): 14–15.

Belanoff, Pat and Peter Elbow. *Sharing and Responding.* NY: McGraw-Hill. 1995.

——. *A Community of Writers: A Workshop Course in Writing.* 2nd ed. NY: McGraw-Hill, 1995.

Berthoff, Ann E. *Forming Thinking Writing: The Composing Imagination.* Rochelle Park: Hayden, 1978.

Bouton, Clark, and Russell Y. Garth, eds. *Learning in Groups.* San Francisco: Jossey Bass, 1983.

Brannon, Lil. "Toward a Theory of Composition." *Perspectives on Research and Scholarship in Composition.* Ben McClelland and Timothy Donovan, eds. New York: MLA, 1988. 6–25.

Bridges, Charles W., ed. *Training the New Teacher of College Composition.* Urbana, IL: NCTE, 1986.

Bruffee, Kenneth. "Collaborative Learning and the 'Conversation of Mankind.'" *CE* 46 (Nov. 1984): 635-52.

→

——. "Teaching Writing Through Collaboration" *Learning in Groups*. Clark Bouton and Russell Y. Garth, eds. San Francisco: Jossey-Bass, 1983.

Bullock, Richard, John Trumber, and Charles Schuster, eds. *The Politics of Writing Instruction: Postsecondary*. Portsmouth, N.H.: Boynton/Cook, 1991.

Capossela, Toni-Lee, ed. *The Critical Writing Workshop: Designing Writing Assignments to Foster Critical Thinking*. Portsmouth, N.H.: Boynton-Cook, 1993.

Christensen, Francis, and Bonniejean Christensen. *A New Rhetoric*. N.Y.: Harper and Row, 1976.

Clark, Beverly Lyon. *Talking about Writing: A Guide for Tutor and Teacher Conferences*. Ann Arbor: U. Of Michigan Press, 1985.

Clifford, John. "Composing in Stages: The Effects of a Collaborative Pedagogy." *RTE* 15 (1981): 37–53.

Connolly, Paul, and Teresa Vilvardi, eds. *New Methods in College Writing Programs: Theories in Practice*. NY: MLA, 1986.

Cooper, Charles, and Lee Odell, eds. *Evaluating Writing: Describing, Measuring, Judging*. Urbana IL: NCTE, 1977.

Cooper, Marilyn, and Michael Holzman, eds. *Writing as Social Action*. Portsmouth, N.H.: Boynton/Cook, 1989.

Corbett, Edward P.J., and Gary Tate, eds. *The Writing Teacher's Sourcebook*. 2nd ed. New York: Oxford U.P., 1988.

Donovan, Timothy R., and Ben W. McClelland, eds. *Eight Approaches to Teaching Composition*. Urbana, IL: NCTE, 1980.

——. *Perspectives on Research and Scholarship in Composition*. NY: MLA, 1985.

Ede, Lisa. *Singular Texts/Plural Authors: Perspectives on Collaborative Writing*. Carbondale: Southern Illinois University Press, 1990.

Elbow, Peter. *Embracing Contraries: Explorations in Learning and Teaching*. NY: Oxford U.P., 1986.

——. *Writing with Power: Techniques for Mastering the Writing Process*. NY: Oxford U.P., 1981.

——. *Writing Without Teachers*. NY: Oxford U.P., 1973.

Flower, Linda. *Problem-Solving Strategies for Writing*. 2nd ed. NY: Harcourt Brace Jovanovich, 1985.

Freedman, Sarah Warshauer, *Response to Student Writing*. Urbana, IL: NCTE, 1987.

Fulkerson, Richard. "Four Philosophies of Composition." *CCC* 30 (Dec 1979): 343–48.

Garrison, Roger. "One to One: Tutorial Instruction in Freshman Composition." *New Directions for Community Colleges* 2 (Spring,1994): 55–84.

Gere, Anne. *Writing Groups: History Theory and Implications*. Carbondale: Southern Illinois University Press, 1987.

Gebhardt, Richard C. "Teamwork and Feedback: Broadening the Base of Collaborative Learning." *CE* 4 (1980):

Golub, Jeff. *Focus on Collaborative Learning*. Urbana, IL: NCTE, 1988.

Haring-Smith, Tori. *Writing Together: Collaborative Learning in the Writing Classroom*. NY: HarperCollins, 1994.

→

——, ed. *A Guide to Writing Programs: Writing Centers, Peer Tutoring, Writing Across the Curriculum.* Glenview: Scott, 1984.

Harris, Muriel. *Teaching One-to-One: The Writing Conference.* Urbana, IL: NCTE, 1986.

Hawkins, Nathaniel. "An Introduction to the History and Theory of Peer Tutoring in Writing." *A Guide to Writing Programs.* Tori Haring-Smith, ed. Glenview: Scott, 1984. 7–18.

Hawkins, Thom. *Group Inquiry Techniques for Teaching Writing.* Urbana, IL: NCTE, 1976.

Healy, Mary K. "Using Student Writing Response Groups in the Classroom." *Teaching Writing.* Gerald Camp., ed. Montclair: Boynton, 1982.

Hillocks, George Jr., *Research on Written Composition: New Directions for Teaching.* Urbana: ERIC Clearinghouse on Reading and Communication Skills, 1986.

Jolliffe, David A. *Writing, Teaching, and Learning: Incorporating Writing Throughout the Curriculum.* NY: HarperCollins, 1997.

Kail, Harvey. "Collaborative Learning in Context: The Problem with Peer Tutoring." *CE* 45 (1983): 592–99.

Kelly, Lou. *From Dialogue to Discourse: An Open Approach to Competence and Creativity.* Glenview: Scott, 1972.

Lamberg, Walter J. "Self-Provided and Peer-Provided Feedback." *CCC.* 31 (1980): 64–69.

LeFevre, Karen Burke. *Invention as a Social Act.* Carbondale: Southern IL UP, 1987.

Lindemann, Erika. *A Rhetoric for Writing Teachers.* 3rd ed. NY: Oxford Univ. Press, 1995.

Macrorie, Ken. *Telling Writing.* 3rd Edition. Rochelle Park: Hayden Book Co., Inc., 1980.

——. *Twenty Teachers.* New York: Oxford U.P., 1984.

Mayer, Emily and Louise Z. Smith. *The Practical Tutor.*

McClelland, Ben, and Timothy O. Donovan, eds. *Eight Approaches to Teaching Composition.* Urbana, IL: NCTE, 1985.

——. *Perspectives on Research and Scholarship in Composition.* NY: MLA, 1985.

Moffett, James. *Teaching the Universe of Discourse.* Boston: Houghton, 1968.

Murray, Donald M. *Learning by Teaching: Selected Articles on Writing and Teaching.* Portsmouth N.H.: Boynton/Cook, 1982.

——. *Expecting the Unexpected: Teaching Myself—and Others—-to Read and Write.* Portsmouth N.H.: Boynton/Cook, 1989.

——. *Classroom Practices in Teaching English.* Focus on Collaborative Learning. Urbana, IL: NCTE, 1988.

Newcomb, Theodore M. "Student Peer Group Influence." *The American College.* Nevitt Sanford, ed. New York: Wiley, 1962.

Newkirk, Thomas. "Direction and Misdirection in Peer Response." CCC 35 (1984): 300–311.

Perl, Sandra. *Landmark Essays on Writing Processes.* NY: Lawrence Erlbaum Associates, Inc., 1994.

Rafoth, Bennett A., and Donald L. Rubin, eds. *The Social Construction of Written Communication.* Norwood, N.J.: Ablex, 1988.

Reid, Joanne, Peter Forrestal, and Jonathan Cook. *Small Group Learning in the Classroom.* Urbana IL: NCTE, 1989.

→

Reither, James A., and Douglas Vipond. "Writing as Collaboration." *CE* 51 (Dec. 1989): 855–867.

Rubin, Donald C. "Introduction: Four Dimensions of Social Construction in Written Communication." *The Social Construction of Written Communication*. Bennett Rafoth and Donald Rubin, eds. 1–33.

Ruggiero, Vincent Ryan. *Enter the Dialogue: A Dramatic Approach to Critical Thinking and Writing*. Belmont, WA: Wadsworth, 1985.

Sommers, Nancy, Donald McQuade, and Michael Tratner, eds. *Student Writers at Work*. NY: St. Martin's Press, 1989.

Spear, Karen. *Sharing Writing: Peer Response Groups in English Classes*. Portsmouth, N.H.: Heinemann, 1988.

Stewart, Donald C. "Collaborative Learning and Composition: Boon or Bane?" *Rhetoric Review* 7 (Fall 1988): 58–85.

Student Writing Groups: Demonstrating the Process. The Workshop Corporation, 1988. Videotape.*

Tate, Gary, ed. *Teaching Composition: Twelve Bibliographical Essays*. Fort Worth: Texas Christian U.P., 1987.

Trimbur, John. "Peer Tutors and the Benefits of Collaborative Learning." *Writing Lab Newsletter* 8 (1983): 109–115.

——. "Collaborative Learning and Teaching Writing." *Perspectives on Research and Scholarship in Composition*. Ben W. McClelland and Timothy R. Donovan, eds. 87–109.

Wagner, Lilya. *Peer Teaching Historical Perspectives*. Westport: Greenwood, 1982.

Webb, Patricia. *Facilitating Peer Response*. Boston: Houghton Mifflin, 1996.

White, Edward M. *Assigning, Responding, Evaluating*: A Writing Teacher's Guide. 3rd ed. N.Y.:St. Martins, 1995.

Writing Across the Curriculum: Longman, 1996. Videotape.*

Writing, Teaching and Learning. Longman, 1996. Videotape.*

Zemelman, Steven and Harvey Danials. *A Community of Writers*. 1988.

*Indicates a videotape: *Student Writing Groups* and *Beginning Writing Groups* are available from The Workshop Corporation, 3832 North Seventh Street, Tacoma, WA 98406. *Writing Across the Curriculum* and *Writing, Teaching and Learning* are available from Longman Publishers at Addison Wesley Longman Publishers, 1185 Avenue of the Americas, 25th Floor, NY, 10011.

WHAT MAKES WRITING GOOD?

(We are not going to presume to know what makes all writing aesthetically pleasing to all people, but there are certain aspects of written English that are essential to academic or university writing. The writing committee at Lehigh University named this list "The Qualities of Effective Expository Writing.")

- **A CLEARLY DEFINED CENTRAL IDEA.** The essay should be on a subject of substance and the central idea should be clear to the reader.

- **STRONG SUPPORT FOR THAT IDEA.** The support may be in the form of personal experience, logical or critical thinking, or the use of textual reference from the works of others.

- **APPROPRIATE ORGANIZATION FOR THAT SUPPORT.** The essay will follow a clear and logical plan of development.

- **COHERENCE.** The essay will be interesting and worth reading. It will teach readers something they did not know or cause them to think in new ways about the subject of the essay.

- **MATURE AND VARIED SENTENCES.** The sentences will be of varied length and format and will avoid triteness and clichés.

- **ATTENTION TO THE CONVENTIONS OF STANDARD WRITTEN ENGLISH.** These conventions include punctuation, word forms, verb tense, subject/verb agreement, spelling, and mechanics.

- **EVIDENCE OF NEATNESS AND CARING.** The essay will look as if it were written by someone who cared enough to develop ideas, spend time on revision, proofread and submit a clean copy.

Courtesy of the Armstrong Atlantic State University Writing Center
Dr. Martha Marinara, Director

CRITERIA FOR "A" LEVEL WRITING FOR ESSAY CONTEST MULTIPLE GENRES

Noteworthy essays engage and maintain readers' interest and also accomplish the writer's purposes with those readers. To achieve those results, essays should demonstrate a high degree of excellence in a majority, if not all, of the following characteristics.

- Create an appropriate and engaging narrative voice that characterizes the writer's involvement with the subject and the audience.

- Reveal issues, ideas, and arguments as the results of rigorous interrogations that challenge fixed assumptions or conventional wisdom.

- Construct significant and powerful central ideas through multiple, often complex, development and persuasive techniques.

- Allow emerging positions to create the shape(s) of the text so form and language derive from the writer's explorations rather than allow prescribed forms to dictate questions or circumscribe ideas.

- Dramatize central ideas through lively language, innovative forms or unusual blending of traditional genres.

- Demonstrate meticulous control of technical and stylistic features as aspects of the writer's craft and as evidence of the writer's investment in the subject and consideration of the audience.

- Demonstrate complete and accurate documentation in appropriate style (MLA usually) as well as consideration for the audience in providing not only the appropriate attributions, correctly cited, but a sensitivity to various techniques for giving credit and providing the reader with information.

Courtesy of the Editorial Board of Watermarks: A Collection of Student Essays
Armstrong Atlantic State Unversity